Pray
Your into Marital
Way BREAK-
THROUGH

2021

A 21-day personal prayer and fasting
Programme to bring change for singles

DR & PASTOR (MRS)
D. K. OLUKOYA

INTRODUCTION

A Special 21-Day Programme for Marital Breakthrough and Deliverance

We praise the matchless name of the Lord because He does wonderful things in this programme every year. We appreciate His faithfulness and the countless testimonies of victory, deliverance and marital breakthrough we record annually. In this year's edition, The God of all possibilities, who changes not, will do marvelous and unsearchable things without number in the lives of His children. The God that answers by fire will visit you and His anointing will break every yoke working against your marital destiny. You will sing your song and dance your marital victory dance, in the name of Jesus.

Luke 21:13 says, "And it shall turn to you for a testimony." Without trials and challenges there will be no testimony. Without fire, there will be no gold. As you fast and pray during this programme, the delay, hindrances and opposition, disappointment, pain and anguish, disfavour, rejection and sorrow you have suffered so far in your quest for marital breakthrough shall turn out as a testimony for you, in the name of Jesus.

Are you finding it difficult to get a suitor? It shall turn to you for a testimony. Have you been jilted once or twice? It shall turn to you for a testimony. Are you advanced in age and getting married looks like an impossible task? It will turn to you for a testimony. Have your enemies told you that you will never get married and have children? It will turn to you for a testimony. Are you unemployed today and need a miracle job? It will turn to you for a testimony. Are you poor and being ridiculed presently? It will turn to you for a testimony in the name of Jesus.

Fasting Instructions

1. You are to break your fast by 2pm each day throughout the period of this programme.
2. We encourage that the prayer routine should be carried out as stated. You should observe your daily vigil prayers from 12 midnight to 12:15 am.

3. To benefit totally, we advise you to read, personalise and make the Bible verses your daily confessions

4. There are personal confessions for each section. After your praise and worship, make the personal confession for the section before you start the prayer each day.

5. The programme shall be rounded off with a marathon prayer meeting with our Father in the Lord, Dr D. K. Olukoya on the last day of the programme, Saturday June 12th, 2021, by 8:00am, at the MFM International Headquarters, Onike, Yaba. It will be streamed live at our major Regional Headquarters nationwide and on all our online platforms.

How to Start and Finish Well

Beloved, for you to get the best results that heaven has prepared for participants in this programme, how you start, go about and finish it matters.

To start the programme on the right foundation, you must make your way right with God. You must accept Jesus as Your

Lord and Saviour. Please, pray this prayer: LORD JESUS, I WANT TO BECOME A CHILD OF GOD. I INVITE YOU INTO EVERY AREA OF MY LFE. I ACCEPT YOU AS MY LORD AND PERSONAL SAVIOUR. FORGIVE MY SINS AND CLEANSE ME WITH YOUR BLOOD. I MAKE A COVENANT TO SERVE YOU FOR THE REST OF MY LIFE. I GIVE MY LIFE TO THE LORDSHIP OF JESUS TODAY AND FOREVER IN JESUS MIGHTY NAME.

If you have said this prayer, I congratulate you as this is a sure foundation for testimonies and miracles for you.

In addition, you need the Holy Spirit and unwavering faith to get the best God has in stock for you in this programme.

This programme is divided into three sections with Scriptures, personal confessions and prayers daily. Please see the different sections below:

Section 1:   HOLY SPIRIT, INCUBATE ME

Section 2:   DESTROYING MARITAL ROAD BLOCKS

Section 3: I WILL SING MY SONG AND DANCE MY MARITAL VICTORY DANCE

Beloved, the God of Elijah will move you out of ridicule and insult and usher you into divine breakthroughs and dumbfounding testimonies, in the mighty name of Jesus.

Kindly share your testimony with us via our emial.
gen218singles@gmail.com

SECTION ONE

PERSONAL CONFESSION

Father, in the name of Jesus, I thank You because You are my Saviour, Father, Protector and Defender. I thank You for the salvation of my soul. My Lord and my God, I appreciate You for You are a covenant keeping God and you have interest in the affairs of my life. My rock and my Shield, I will bless you at all times and your praises shall continually be in my mouth (Psalm 34).

I am not what my circumstances says I am. I am not what mockers or scorners says I am. I am not what the society says I am. I am not a picture of what the national economy and institutionalized wickedness has restructured people to be. I am not what I think I am, but I am what the word of God says I am. I am an express image of Jehovah God on earth, I am fashioned after the likeness of the Creator of the heaven and earth.

I am regenerated by the blood of Jesus. The word of God says I am a royal priesthood I am a holy nation. I am a peculiar person and I am special in the sight of God. The grace of God is upon my life. As the light of His glory, I am full of divine favour, and I am a partaker of all heaven's spiritual blessings.

The Bible says because I believe and receive Jesus Christ, power has been given to me to become a son of God and I am empowered to trample upon serpents and scorpions and all the power of the enemy. Therefore, let no man trouble me, for I bear in my body the mark of the Lord Jesus Christ.

I make these confessions in the name of the Father, in the name of the Son and in the name of the Holy Spirit. Amen!!!

HOLY SPIRIT INCUBATE ME

Date: Sunday 23rd May, 2021

Scripture: John 5:21

Confession: Matthew 3:11-12

Tick after praying morning session:

Tick after praying vigil session:

PRAYERS FOR MORNING SESSION

1. Father, in the name of Jesus, I thank you from the bottom of my heart for what you are going to do in my life through this programme.

2. I cover myself with the blood of Jesus.

3. Holy Spirit, cleanse all soiled parts of my marital life, in the name of Jesus

4. Holy Spirit, refresh every dry area of my marital life, in the name of Jesus.

5. Holy Spirit heal every wounded part of my life, in the name of Jesus

6. Holy Spirit, bend every evil rigidity in my life, in the name of Jesus

7. Holy Spirit, glue me together where I am opposed to myself, in the name of Jesus

8. Holy Spirit, quicken me and increase my desire for the things of heaven, in the name of Jesus

9. By Your rulership, O Lord, let the lust of the flesh in my life die, in the name of Jesus

10. Lord Jesus, increase daily in my life, in the name of Jesus.

VIGIL PRAYERS

11. O Lord, refine and purge my life with your fire, in the name of Jesus.

12. Let your heat, O Lord, consume every invisible hand oppressing my life, in the name of Jesus.

13. Anything within me, preventing the

incubation of the Holy Ghost, catch fire, in the name of Jesus.

14. Lord, plant good things in me and safeguard them with the Holy Ghost fire, in the name of Jesus.

15. Foundational problem in my life that is preventing the incubation of the Holy Spirit, die, in the name of Jesus.

16. Holy Ghost fire, incubate me now, in the name of Jesus (say this 21 times).

17. Holy Spirit, give me divine prescriptions to my marital problems in the name of Jesus.

18. Holy Spirit, help me to locate the defects in the clay of my life, in the name of Jesus.

19. Wherever I am leaking away spiritually, O Lord, seal me up, in the name of Jesus.

20. Begin to thank the Lord for answers to your prayers.

HOLY SPIRIT INCUBATE ME

Date: Monday 24th May, 2021

Scripture: John 5:21

Confession: Romans 14:17

Tick after praying morning session:

Tick after praying vigil session:

PRAYERS FOR MORNING SESSION

21. I cover my body, soul and spirit with the blood of Jesus.

22. Holy Spirit, quicken me and increase my desire for the things of heaven, in the name of Jesus

23. Father Lord, breathe your life-giving breath into my soul, in the name of Jesus

24. Lord Jesus, come like blood into my veins, in the name of Jesus

25. Holy Ghost, let Your fire, generate power in my life, in the name of Jesus

26. Holy Spirit, come as dew and refresh me, in the name of Jesus

27. Holy Spirit, guide me in the way of marital breakthrough, in the name of Jesus

28. Holy Spirit, where my love is cold, warm me up, in the name of Jesus

29. Holy Spirit, purify the channel of my life, in the name of Jesus

30. Begin to thank God for answers to prayers, in the name of Jesus

VIGIL PRAYERS

31. O Lord, kindle in me the fire of charity, in the name of Jesus

32. Holy Spirit, control my ability to frame my words, in the name of Jesus

33. O Lord, let the spirit that flees from sin, incubate my life, in the name of Jesus

34. I renounce my rights to anger, in the name of Jesus

35. Super blood of Jesus, sanitise my spirit man, in the name of Jesus

36. Holy Spirit, add flavour to my life, in the name of Jesus

37. I am available Holy Spirit, turn me to unquenchable fire, in the name of Jesus

38. I need direction, Holy Spirit lead me through my journey for marital breakthrough, in the name of Jesus

39. I shall prevail with man and with God, in the name of Jesus.

40. Thank the Lord for speedy answers to your prayers, in the name of Jesus

Section One: Day Three

HOLY SPIRIT INCUBATE ME

Date: Tuesday 25th May, 2021

Scripture: Mathew 3:11-12

Confession: Philippines 4:13

Tick after praying morning session:

Tick after praying vigil session:

PRAYERS FOR MORNING SESSION

41. Thank God for the purifying power of the fire of the Holy Ghost

42. I release my life from every character and negative anointing, in the name of Jesus

43. I challenge every organ of my body with the fire of the Holy Spirit, in the name of Jesus

44. Let every human spirit attacking my spirit, release me, in the name of Jesus

45. Baptism of the Holy Ghost, enter into my spirit, in the name of Jesus.

46. Baptism of the Holy Ghost with fire, overshadow my life, in the name of Jesus.

47. Holy Ghost, burn every chaff in my life with Your fire, in the name of Jesus.

48. Holy Ghost, thoroughly purge my life, in the name of Jesus.

49. I shall walk every day in victory and liberty of spirit, in the name of Jesus

50. Holy Spirit, take over my day and turn it to testimonies, in the name of Jesus

VIGIL PRAYERS

51. O God, arise and uproot anything you have not planted in my life, in the name of Jesus.

52. Every wicked altar in my spirit, I throw you down, in the name of Jesus

53. O Lord, empower my spirit with your authority, in the name of Jesus

54. O Lord, take me from where I am now to

where you want me to be, in the name of Jesus

55. I reject dryness in my walk with God, in the name of Jesus

56. I overcome powerlessness and confusion, in the name of Jesus

57. Poison of powerlessness in my spirit, be neutralised, in the name of Jesus

58. The desire of the enemies to harvest my soul shall not prosper, in the name of Jesus

59. Let my point of ridicule be converted to a source of miracle, in the name of Jesus

60. Spend quality time to bless the name of the Lord.

Section One: Day Four

HOLY SPIRIT INCUBATE ME

Date: Wednesday 26th May, 2021

Scripture: 1 Samuel 2:3

Confession: Philippines 2:9

Tick after praying morning session:

Tick after praying vigil session:

PRAYERS FOR MORNING SESSION

61. O Lord, ignite Your gift of discernment in me, in the name of Jesus

62. Let my spiritual sight and eardrums receive healing, in the name of Jesus

63. O Lord, quicken my spiritual sensitivity, in the name of Jesus.

64. O Lord, produce in me the power of self control and gentleness, in the name of Jesus

65. You powers that quenched the fire of God in people's lives, I am not your candidate, loose your hold over my life in the name of Jesus.

66. Lord, give me the name that will bless me today, in the name of Jesus.

67. O Lord, deliver me from every satanic noise, in the name of Jesus.

68. O Lord, deliver me from every satanic distraction in the name of Jesus.

69. The Lord will not be a spectator over my affairs, but a major participant, in the name of Jesus

70. O Lord, anchor Your mercy to my head, in the name of Jesus

VIGIL PRAYERS

71. I release every faculty of my life from the dominion of Mr Flesh, in the name of Jesus

72. Let God be God in the manifestation of my marital breakthrough, in the name of Jesus

73. Anointing of desert spirit in my life, dry up by fire, in the name of Jesus

74. My head, refuse to bear any evil burden, in the name of Jesus

75. Any power that has been supplying strength to weaknesses in my spirit man, die, in the name of Jesus

76. I refuse to be kept busy by the devil, in the name of Jesus

77. The enemies shall not understand the issues of my life, in the name of Jesus

78. I reject the spirit of stagnation and marital delay, in the name of Jesus

79. My life shall not be hung on the shelf, in the name of Jesus

80. Every power set up to pull me down spiritually, be disgraced, in the name of Jesus.

Section One: Day Five

HOLY SPIRIT INCUBATE ME

Date: Thursday 27th May, 2021

Scripture: Psalm 19:1-14

Confession: Isaiah 43:19

Tick after praying morning session:

Tick after praying vigil session:

PRAYERS FOR MORNING SESSION

81. My prayers will bring me my marital testimony in this programme, in the name of Jesus

82. I dismantle any power working against my efficiency, in the name of Jesus

83. I refuse to lock the door of divine visitation against myself, in the name of Jesus.

84. I receive heavenly resources into my spirit today for the production of my marital breakthrough, in the name of Jesus

85. My life magnetise the Holy Ghost fire, in the name of Jesus.

86. All my departed glory, hear the word of the Lord, be restored now, in the name of Jesus.

87. Ministering Angels, set my life on track for destiny fulfilment, in the name of Jesus.

88. Anyone occupying my seat of honour, clear away, in the name of Jesus.

89. O Lord, give me a marital testimony that will give birth to other testimonies, in the name of Jesus

90. O Lord, make me a reference point of divine blessing, in the name of Jesus

VIGIL PRAYERS

91. Holy Ghost, bombard my life with divine helpers, in the name of Jesus

92. I refuse to get stuck on one level of spiritual growth, in the name of Jesus

93. Every good thing that I ever seek, Holy Ghost possess them for me, in the name of Jesus

94. Let the garden of my life yield super abundance, in the name of Jesus

95. Ugly feet, walk out of my marital life, in the name of Jesus

96. Every spiritual leprosy in my life, catch fire, in the name of Jesus

97. Lead me, O Lord, to my own Land that flows with milk and honey, in the name of Jesus

98. I destroy every clock and time table of the enemy for my marital life, in the name of Jesus

99. Holy Spirit, direct my mind, in the name of Jesus

100. Holy Spirit, do the work of deliverance in my life today, in the name of Jesus.

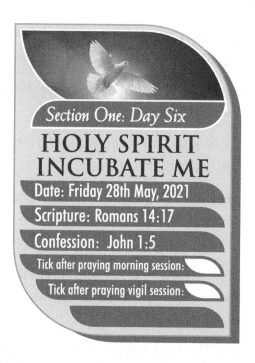

HOLY SPIRIT INCUBATE ME

Date: Friday 28th May, 2021

Scripture: Romans 14:17

Confession: John 1:5

Tick after praying morning session:

Tick after praying vigil session:

PRAYERS FOR MORNING SESSION

101. Righteousness, peace, joy in the Holy Ghost, overshadow my life today, in the name of Jesus

102. Glory of my marriage, appear, manifest now, in the name of Jesus

103. Spirit of impossibility, jump out of my marital life now, in the name of Jesus.

104. Fire of God, heal my spiritual injury, in the name of Jesus

105. I refuse to be an object for satanic

transactions, in the name of Jesus.

106. Profitless hard work pack your load and get out of my life, in the name of Jesus.

107. Anointing for profit-yielding ideas, fall upon my life, in the name of Jesus.

108. Let all my mistakes be converted to miracles, in the name of Jesus.

109. O Lord, close the gap between where I am and where You want me to be, in the name of Jesus

110. I receive angelic assistance today, for my marital breakthrough, in the name of Jesus

VIGIL PRAYERS

111. O Lord, illuminate Your truth to my understanding, in the name of Jesus

112. Lord, let me, with the eyes of my heart, see You clearly, in the name of Jesus

113. Lord, separate me from marital woes, in the name of Jesus

114. I separate myself from satan and his kingdom, in the name of Jesus

115. I renounce the kingdom of darkness and embrace the kingdom of Jesus Christ

116. Lord Jesus, deliver me from evil marital delay, in the name of Jesus

117. My destiny is attached to God; therefore, I decree that I can never fail, in the name of Jesus

118. I reject every satanic alternative for my marital destiny, in the name of Jesus

119. O Lord, anoint my destiny afresh, in the name of Jesus

120. I have come to Zion, my marital breakthrough must manifest this year, in the name of Jesus.

HOLY SPIRIT INCUBATE ME

Date: Saturday 29th May, 2021

Scripture: Isaiah 43:1

Confession: Luke 1:35

Tick after praying morning session:

Tick after praying vigil session:

PRAYERS FOR MORNING SESSION

121. My life shall not suffer affliction, in the name of Jesus

122. Let my divine destiny appear, let my perverted destiny disappear, in the name of Jesus

123. Every damage done to my marital destiny, Holy Spirit repair it, in the name of Jesus.

124. I refuse to operate below my divine destiny, in the name of Jesus

125. The desire of my enemies will not be granted over my marital life, in the name of Jesus.

126. Those who once mocked me shall not witness my glorious marriage, in the name of Jesus.

127. O Lord, give me new eyes to see into my destiny, in the name of Jesus.

128. I enter into my prophetic destiny by fire, in the name of Jesus.

129. The leaf of my marital destiny shall not wither, in the name of Jesus

130. Every attack against my marital destiny when I was a child, be destroyed, in the name of Jesus

VIGIL PRAYERS

131. O Lord, reschedule my destiny for uncommon visitation, in the name of Jesus

132. O Lord, renew my strength, in the name of Jesus

133. O Lord, deliver me from the lies that I tell myself, in the name of Jesus

134. Holy Spirit, rain on me now rain of marital favor, in the name of Jesus

135. Holy Spirit, open my eyes to see behind the visible to the invisible, in the name of Jesus

136. Let my point of ridicule be converted to my source of miracles, in the name of Jesus

137. In the presence of those laughing me to scorn, my marital testimonies appear by fire, in the name of Jesus

138. O Lord, anoint my eyes, hands and legs to locate my divine partner, in the name of Jesus

139. Every problem that came into my life by personal invitation, depart now, in the name of Jesus

140. Thank God for answers to your prayers.

SECTION TWO

Father, in the name of Jesus, I thank You for all you have been doing in my marital life since this programme started. I believe that You are my God and You are working out my marital celebration already. Please, accept my thanksgiving, in the name of Jesus.

The Lord will perfect all that concerns me; He will not forsake me because His mercy endures forever. I will not be disappointed at the edge of my marital breakthrough. The marital good works that He has started in my life, Jesus will finish them, because He is the Alpha and Omega and He does not leave things half done. My Saviour completes and perfects everything He starts.

Lord Jesus, hear me speedily. Hasten Your word to perform Your wonderful promises for my marital life. God is not a man that He should lie nor the Son of Man that He should repent of any of His pronouncements. I believe that every promise of God for my life shall come to pass without any satanic delay.

I stand on the victory of Jesus over satan and over death and hell. For it is written that Jesus first of all descended into the lower parts of the earth and stripped the devil of all his powers and ascended on high, leading captivity captive. By this victory, let every stumbling block, every gathering of powers of darkness and every satanic bus stop delaying the manifestation of my marital congratulations be destroyed now by the power in the blood of Jesus.

In the presence of those who have written me off, the zeal of God shall bring forth my marital celebration. I refuse to give up on my marriage because God has not given up on me. My God is preparing a giant marital testimony for me and His covenant shall bring it to manifestation this season. What I confess is what I attract.

I make these confessions in the name of the Father, in the name of the Son and in the name of the Holy Spirit. Amen!!!

DESTROYING MARITAL ROAD BLOCKS

Date: Sunday 30th May, 2021

Scripture: Psalm 91: 1-16

Confession: 1 John 2:8

Tick after praying morning session:

Tick after praying vigil session:

PRAYERS FOR MORNING SESSION

1. You, the marine powers claiming right over my life and marriage, loose your hold and die, in the name of Jesus.

2. Every spirit that entered me through curses, go out now, in the name of Jesus.

3. Legal right of satanic harassment over my marriage, break, in the name of Jesus

4. I break the pattern of darkness locking me up maritally, in the name of Jesus.

5. Any power from the water, programmed against my marriage, die, in the name of Jesus.

6. Power from the sea, release my marriage now, in the name of Jesus.

7. Marine spirits, release my marital blessings by fire, in the name of Jesus.

8. Marine spirits, release my marital potential by fire, in the name of Jesus.

9. Marine spirits, release my head by fire, in the name of Jesus.

10. Holy Ghost fire, destroy every satanic anti-marriage garment in my life, in the name of Jesus.

VIGIL PRAYERS

11. Marine spirits, release my womb by fire, in the name of Jesus.

12. Marine spirits, release my reproductive organ by fire, in the name of Jesus.

13. Marine spirits, release my children by fire, in the name of Jesus.

14. O Lord, lay your hand upon me and quench

every rebellion in my marriage, in the name of Jesus.

15. Problems (name them) harassing my life, I break your backbone by fire, in the name of Jesus.

16. You, my marriage inside the water, catch fire and locate me now, in the name of Jesus.

17. Every demonic antenna magnetizing marital disfavour in my life, be dismantled by fire of God, in the name of Jesus.

18. I release my life by fire from the hold of snail and tortoise anointing on my marital situation, in the name of Jesus.

19. Every activity of jealousy and envy fashioned against my life, be disgraced and be dismantled now by the blood of Jesus

20. Every evil wall of partition between me and my divine partner, be scattered by the fire of God.

DESTROYING MARITAL ROAD BLOCKS

Date: Monday 31st May, 2021

Scripture: Psalm 130: 1-8

Confession: Galatians 3: 13-15

Tick after praying morning session:

Tick after praying vigil session:

PRAYERS FOR MORNING SESSION

1. You, devil, take your legs and hands away from me and my ordained partner in the name of Jesus.

2. Every stronghold of thought, image and pictures of marital failure in my heart, be pulled down by fire, in the name of Jesus.

3. I reject every spirit of doubt, fear and discouragement maritally, in the name of Jesus.

4. Let all the demonic obstacles that have been established in the heart of my ordained

partner against my marriage be destroyed, in the name of Jesus.

5. Lord, always help me to identify evil marital traps, in the name of Jesus.

6. You, unfriendly friends, I command you, depart from me, in the name of Jesus.

7. Let every power chasing away my partner, be paralysed, in the name of Jesus.

8. Every witchcraft power working against my marital fulfilment fall down and die, in the name of Jesus.

9. The enemy of my marriage will not convert my destiny to rags, in the name of Jesus.

10. Every incantation and ritual working against my marriage, be disgraced, in the name of Jesus.

VIGIL PAYERS

11. Satan, I resist and rebuke your effort to change my marital destiny, in the name of Jesus.

12. Every incantation, ritual and witchcraft power against my marriage, fall down and die, in the name of Jesus.

13. I dash every evil clock controlling my life on the wall of fire, in the name of Jesus.

14. By the power in the blood of Jesus, I command all dreams and visions concerning my marital life that have been amputated to receive divine strength, in the name of Jesus.

15. Agent from the marine kingdom assigned to block my marriage, be disgraced by the fire of God, in the name of Jesus.

16. Every padlock-spirit against my marriage, give way by the spirit of God in Jesus name.

17. Every evil curse/covenant against fulfilling my marital destiny, break by the fire and thunder of God, in the name of Jesus.

18. Every mountain of satanic confrontation in every department of my life, crumble now, in the name of Jesus.

19. I render every Goliath defying my prayers impotent, in the name of Jesus.

20. Every satanic manipulation aimed at changing my marital destiny, be frustrated, in the name of Jesus.

Section Two: Day Three

DESTROYING MARITAL ROAD BLOCKS

Date: Tuesday 1st June, 2021

Scripture: Psalm 135: 1-21

Confession: Philippians 2:9-11

Tick after praying morning session:

Tick after praying vigil session:

PRAYERS FOR MORNING SESSION

1. Every terrible covenant organised against my marriage, scatter, in the name of Jesus.

2. After the order of Moses, I raise up my staff of prayer to divide my marital Red Sea, in the name of Jesus.

3. Every robber of my marital favour, die, in the name of Jesus.

4. Every affliction targeted at the edge of my marital breakthrough, die, in the name of Jesus.

5. Let God arise in his anger and fight my marital war for me, in the name of Jesus

6. Let every anti-marriage altar fashioned against me be destroyed with the fire of God, in the name of Jesus.

7. O Lord, give me the power to dismantle every marital obstacle, in the name of Jesus.

8. I clear my marital shoes and gown from the warehouse of the strong man, in the name of Jesus.

9. You, child of the devil occupying my marital seat, clear away, in the name of Jesus.

10. I refuse to pick my spouse from the camp of the enemy.

VIGIL PRAYERS

11. Let evil hands be removed from my marital miracles, in the name of Jesus.

12. Let the arrow of the Lord be strong in the heart of my marital enemies, in the name of Jesus.

13. You marine powers that are monitoring my life and marriage, I bring the hook and the rebuke of the Lord upon you, and I anchor

your head to divine judgement, in the name of Jesus

14. Jesus is my original spouse and is jealous over me; therefore, I issue a bill of divorcement to every spirit wife/husband, in the name of Jesus.

15. Let heavenly testimony overcome every testimony of hell in my life, in the name of Jesus.

16. I release the fire of God on my evil regalia, in the name of Jesus.

17. Let all evil chiefs and guard servants in any kingdom be consumed by fire, in the name of Jesus.

18. Let every evil mark of failure in marital relationship upon me, be removed by the blood of Jesus.

19. I release myself from the prison of spiritual husband/wife and marriage, in the name of Jesus.

20. I demolish and pull down the walls of evil thoughts and anger in me, by fire, in the name of Jesus.

DESTROYING MARITAL ROAD BLOCKS

Date: Wednesday 2nd June, 2021

Scripture: Psalm 136: 1-26

Confession: Isaiah 54:14-15

Tick after praying morning session:

Tick after praying vigil session:

PRAYERS FOR MORNING SESSION

1. Let my spiritual husband/wife be roasted by the fire of God, in the name of Jesus.

2. I rebuke the activities of the emptier over my home, in the name of Jesus.

3. Every power walking about in the dark, in order to harm me, be bound and be paralysed, in the name of Jesus.

4. I bind the evil spirit working in support of the enemies of my marriage in Jesus name.

5. Powers or evil personalities observing sleepless nights for the sake of my marriage, fall down and die, in the name of Jesus.

6. O Lord, shape my life to the right place, in the name of Jesus.

7. Let the Lord God of Elijah arise with a strong hand against every spirit husband /wife and power of the dog, in the name of Jesus.

8. I command every plantation of the dog in my life to come out with all its roots, in the name of Jesus.

9. Let my eyes be delivered from lustfulness, in the name of Jesus.

10. I release myself from every dream pollution, in the name of Jesus.

VIGIL PRAYERS

11. I break the stronghold of marital curses in my life, in the name of Jesus.

12. Any tree harboring any charm against me, receive the fresh fire of God and be roasted, in the name of Jesus.

13. I command all demonic hindrances to my marriage to scatter, in the name of Jesus.

14. O Lord, let every demonic stronghold keeping my marriage in bondage release me and be destroyed, in the name of Jesus.

15. I break and loose myself from every spell of marital bondage and delay, in the name of Jesus.

16. I release myself from every conscious and unconscious covenant with the spirit of marital failure, in the name of Jesus.

17. I release my marriage from the ditch of marriage destroyers, in the name of Jesus.

18. O Lord, let all marital hindrances be removed, in the name of Jesus.

19. I remove my name and partner's name from the book of marital failure, in the name of Jesus.

20. O Lord, let my marriage become too hot to handle for demonic agents, in the name of Jesus.

Section Two: Day Five

DESTROYING MARITAL ROAD BLOCKS

Date: Thursday 3rd June, 2021

Scripture: Psalm 140: 1-13

Confession: Isaiah 54:17

Tick after praying morning session:

Tick after praying vigil session:

PRAYERS FOR MORNING SESSION

1. O Lord, let every satanic angel diverting my marriage partner from me be paralysed, in the name of Jesus.

2. I bind every anti-marriage force, in the name of Jesus.

3. O Lord, let every spirit of demonic delay and marital hindrances be rendered impotent, in the name of Jesus.

4. I receive the mandate to fight every enemy of my marital breakthrough, in the name of Jesus.

5. O Lord, help me to identify and deal with any weakness in me that can hinder my marital breakthroughs, in the name of Jesus.

6. You devil, take your legs away from my marital affairs, in the name of Jesus.

7. Every evil directed at my marriage, backfire, in the name of Jesus.

8. Every inherited demonic deposit working against my marital success, be flushed out by the blood of Jesus.

9. I pull down every demonic stronghold rising up against me, in the name of Jesus.

10. Every effect of parental curses upon my marriage, be cancelled by the blood of Jesus.

VIGIL PRAYERS

11. Every effect of demonic initiation upon my marital destiny, be cancelled by the blood of Jesus.

12. Every effect of any demonic marriage upon my marital destiny, be cancelled by the blood of Jesus.

13. Every effect of demonic alteration of marital destiny upon my life, be cancelled by the blood of Jesus.

14. I release myself from every evil marital bondage, in the name of Jesus.

15. Anti-marriage spells and curses working against my destiny, be broken in the name of Jesus.

16. Bondage and bewitchment fashioned against my settling down in marriage, be broken in the name of Jesus.

17. Every attack of my marital goodness through cobweb, fall down and die, in the name of Jesus

18. I paralyse the handiwork of household enemies and envious agents concerning my marital life, in the name of Jesus.

19. Every evil spiritual wedding conducted consciously or unconsciously on my behalf, die, in the name of Jesus.

20. Mercy of God, favour of God, bring forth my marriage, in the name of Jesus.

Section Two: Day Six

DESTROYING MARITAL ROAD BLOCKS

Date: Friday 4th June, 2021

Scripture: Psalm 141: 1-10

Confession: Proverb 26:27

Tick after praying morning session:

Tick after praying vigil session:

PRAYERS FOR MORNING SESSION

1. O Lord, let every enchantment, divination, incantation, working against my settling down in marriage, die, in the name of Jesus.

2. Every demonic power hindering my marital breakthrough, be frustrated, in the name of Jesus.

3. Every human agent hindering and working against my marriage, be exposed and catch fire, in the name of Jesus.

4. I command all evil marks and labels in my life to be erased by the blood of Jesus.

5. I reject every evil spiritual marriage contamination, in the name of Jesus.

6. I release myself from the spirit of marital bitterness, in the name of Jesus.

7. Every hold of the power of familiar spirit on my marriage, die, in the name of Jesus.

8. O Lord, I refuse to live under any satanic cloud, in the name of Jesus.

9. Any battle that is older than me, causing me marital delay, Rock of Ages, crush them away, in the name of Jesus.

10. Let every geographical hindrance to my marital breakthrough clear away, in the name of Jesus.

VIGIL PRAYERS

11. Every power tying me down, fall down and die, in the name of Jesus.

12. Every power stealing from me, fall down and die, in the name of Jesus.

13. Every gathering of the ungodly against me, maritally, be scattered unto desolation, in the name of Jesus.

14. I dismantle, by fire, the consequences of every satanic spiritual cobweb upon my life and marriage, in the name of Jesus.

15. O Lord, give me the power to overcome negative addictions in my life and marriage, in the name of Jesus.

16. I vomit every evil consumption in the dream, in the name of Jesus.

17. Let any man or woman observing my marriage in the day and night for evil be tortured by fire.

18. Every spirit behind any evil addiction or habit in my life, be bound, in the name of Jesus.

19. Every hand that feeds me in the dream, be roasted by fire, in the name of Jesus.

20. Every power that has turned my sleep to a battle ground, scatter and die, in the name of Jesus.

DESTROYING MARITAL ROAD BLOCKS

Date: Saturday 5th June, 2021

Scripture: Psalm 142:1-7

Confession: Psalm 105: 14-15

Tick after praying morning session:

Tick after praying vigil session:

PRAYERS FOR MORNING SESSION

1. I blind every witchcraft-sponsored infirmity and I cast them out, in the name of Jesus.

2. Every charm working against my marriage, be destroyed, in the name of Jesus.

3. Every device of darkness that is troubling my marriage, be destroyed, in the name of Jesus.

4. Every satanic priesthood manipulating my marital life, be disgraced, in the name of Jesus.

5. I dethrone all human and satanic princes that are assigned to cage my marriage, in the name of Jesus.

6. I bind every power of astral attack assigned against my marriage, in the name of Jesus.

7. I come against every altar or shrine of darkness working against my marriage, in the name of Jesus.

8. Every satanic injection working against my destiny and marital life, backfire, in the name of Jesus.

9. (Place your hand on your head) Every sickness from the dream that fights before and after marriage, get out now, in the name of Jesus.

10. I break every bewitchment pot over my marital life, in the name of Jesus.

VIGIL PRAYERS

11. Every witchcraft power that has introduced spirit husband/wife or children into my marital life, be roasted by fire, in the name of Jesus.

12. Every agent of witchcraft physically attached to my marital life to frustrate it,

fall down and perish, in the name of Jesus.

13. I loose my mind, soul and marital life from the bondage of marine witches, in the name of Jesus.

14. Every arrow shot into my life from under the waters through witchcraft, come out of me and go back to your sender, in the name of Jesus.

15. I destroy the hand of any witch doctor working against my marital life, in the name of Jesus.

16. Let the brush of the Lord scrub out every dirtiness in my spiritual pipe, in the name of Jesus.

17. O Lord, empower me to resist satan so that he would flee, in the name of Jesus.

18. I send the fire of God to my ears and eyes to melt away satanic deposit, in the name of Jesus.

19. Let the blood of Jesus remove any unprogressive label from every aspect of my life, in the name of Jesus.

20. Anti-marriage breakthrough decrees, be revoked, in the name of Jesus.

SECTION THREE

As I make this confession, I declare to the devil that I am not ignorant of who I am in Christ. I am born again and I belong to God. Jesus bought me with His precious and blameless blood and He has translated my life from the kingdom of darkness into His kingdom of light.

I confess and decree that this is my season of marital celebration. The Lord will have mercy on me. My Saviour will shower me with His favour for marital breakthrough that will make me forget my past tears. I do not have any reason to worry because my God will never come late in my case.

I am peculiar and unique. My story will end in glory. My God has the final say and He will make me to laugh last over my marital foes.

I begin to prophetically dance the way I would dance on my wedding day. I will sing for joy and my joy shall be full. This is my season, my time has come. My marriage shall be fruitful, I shall not have delay in child bearing. The Lord has counted me worthy among those who will get married this year. I may not understand how it will happen but my God will bring it to pass because He is a mysterious God. His ways are different from those of men.

Some trust in chariots. Some trust in horses. Some trust in other gods and some trust in their wisdom, but I put my trust in the name of the Lord. I have faith in God because He has never failed and He will never fail. I am blessed, my life partner is blessed, my marriage is blessed, and the children that God will give me are blessed. I will be a source of blessing to my life partner. I shall live long to enjoy my marriage in good health and prosperity. And by this time next year, my marital status would have changed; my testimony will be full and complete. The God of Israel will bless me maritally without adding any sorrow, in the name of Jesus.

I make the confession, in the name of the Father, the Son and the Holy Spirit. Amen!!!!

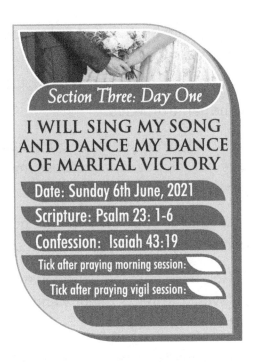

Section Three: Day One

I WILL SING MY SONG AND DANCE MY DANCE OF MARITAL VICTORY

Date: Sunday 6th June, 2021

Scripture: Psalm 23: 1-6

Confession: Isaiah 43:19

Tick after praying morning session:

Tick after praying vigil session:

PRAYERS FOR MORNING SESSION

1. O Lion of Judah, swallow every power attacking the peace in my relationship, in the name of Jesus.

2. My life will not regret serving Jesus, in the name of Jesus.

3. O Lord, purify the channels of my life, in the name of Jesus.

4. Let your heat, O Lord, consume my will, maritally, in the name of Jesus.

5. Let your fire burn all that is not holy in my life, in the name of Jesus.

6. Holy Spirit, come as dew and refresh me, in the name of Jesus.

7. Blood of Jesus, enter into my body and give me the power to possess my marital possession, in the name of Jesus

8. Anointing to reach my marital goals, fall upon me by fire, in the name of Jesus.

9. O God my Father, gather people together to favour me in this country and abroad, in the name of Jesus.

10. O God, arise and use my life to surprise my enemies, in the name of Jesus.

VIGIL PRAYERS

11. Father Lord, release Your dew of heaven upon every dry situation in my life, in the name of Jesus.

12. Father Lord, deposit the magnet of marital favour and prosperity in my life, in the name of Jesus.

13. O Lord my Father, remember me for good

maritally and begin to manifest in my life by Your name called wonderful, in the name of Jesus.

14. Blood of Jesus Christ of Nazareth, speak peace between me and my divinely ordained partner, in the name of Jesus.

15. All ungodly delay to the manifestations of my marital miracles, scatter, in the name of Jesus.

16. I bind and cast out of my life, every spirit of marital limitation, in the name of Jesus.

17. I bind and cast out of my life, every spirit of marital frustration, in the name of Jesus.

18. Lord, show my ordained partner the dreams, vision and restlessness and courage that would advance my cause, in the name of Jesus

19. Attack on my finances because of my marital plans, fail, in the name of Jesus.

20. Lord, let me be at the right place at the right time maritally, in the name of Jesus.

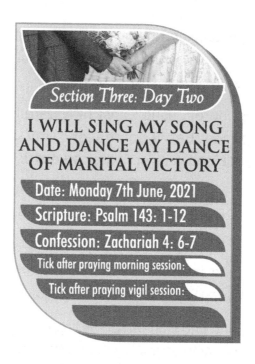

Section Three: Day Two

I WILL SING MY SONG AND DANCE MY DANCE OF MARITAL VICTORY

Date: Monday 7th June, 2021

Scripture: Psalm 143: 1-12

Confession: Zachariah 4: 6-7

Tick after praying morning session:

Tick after praying vigil session:

PRAYERS FOR MORNING SESSION

1. O Lord, anytime I want to make marital mistake, redirect me aright, in the name of Jesus

2. I refuse to marry below my divine destiny, in the name of Jesus.

3. O Lord, anoint my eyes, hands and legs to locate my divine purpose. in the name of Jesus.

4. O Lord, anoint my eyes, hands and legs to locate my divine partner, in the name of Jesus

5. Holy Spirit, I invite you into my imagination, guide me, in the name of Jesus.

6. I receive explosive marital breakthroughs; I reject weak marital breakthroughs, in the name of Jesus.

7. O Lord, shake me to sense where I have made mistakes, in the name of Jesus.

8. Testimonies that are greater than my age, baptise me now, in the name of Jesus.

9. O God, arise and give me a miracle that will announce me to the whole world, in the name of Jesus.

10. Every satanic stabilizer programmed into my progress against fulfilling my divine destiny, be scattered to nothing, in the name of Jesus.

VIGIL PRAYERS

11. O Lord, begin to convert my marital mockery to advancement, in the name of Jesus.

12. I refuse to ask in contrast to God's will for my marriage, in the name of Jesus.

13. Every demonic reverse gear assigned to hinder my marital progress, catch fire, in the name of Jesus.

14. My Father, uphold me with Your right hand of righteousness so as not to fall physically or spiritually, in the name of Jesus.

15. My eyes, reject marital blindness, in the name of Jesus.

16. Let all anti-breakthrough designs against my life and marriage be shattered to irreparable pieces, in the name of Jesus.

17. Let every power chasing marital blessings away from me be paralysed, in the name of Jesus.

18. My Father, let me walk into my marital timing, in the name of Jesus.

19. My days, cooperate with the Almighty, in the name of Jesus.

20. Multiple river of income and cash, locate my life, in the name of Jesus.

Section Three: Day Three

I WILL SING MY SONG AND DANCE MY DANCE OF MARITAL VICTORY

Date: Tuesday 8th June, 2021

Scripture: Psalm 145:1-21

Confession: Acts 10:38

Tick after praying morning session:

Tick after praying vigil session:

PRAYERS FOR MORNING SESSION

1. Power of greatness, come upon my life, in the name of Jesus.

2. Power of knowledge, come upon my life, in the name of Jesus.

3. Power of great opportunities, come upon my life, in the name of Jesus.

4. My divine marital joy, manifest by fire, in the name of Jesus.

5. O God of Elijah, answer my prayer by fire, in the name of Jesus.

6. Let the counsel of God prosper in my life and marriage in the name of Jesus.

7. Let the angels of God begin to work on my marriage, in the name of Jesus.

8. I break the stronghold of pride in my life in the name of Jesus.

9. As from today, my eyes, be controlled by the Holy Spirit, in Jesus name.

10. My marital life, receive the favour and the blessing of God, in the name of Jesus.

VIGIL PRAYERS

11. Every stranger that wants to steal my love from the heart of my partner, catch fire, in the name of Jesus

12. Oh God, arise and let every enemy of my marital breakthrough be scattered, in the name of Jesus.

13. Oh Lord, baptize me with the spirit of favour, in the name of Jesus.

14. Holy Spirit, be my guide in choosing a life partner, in the name of Jesus.

15. I reject every spirit of marital frustration. in the name of Jesus

16. Oh Lord, let the joy of the enemy over my marital life be converted to sorrow, in the name of Jesus.

17. I loose angels, to go and create breakthrough for my marriage, in the name of Jesus.

18. You spirit of strive and anger, I bind and render you to naught in my life, in the name of Jesus.

19. O Lord, everything the enemy has said is impossible in my marriage, make them possible, in the name of Jesus.

20. I release myself into my marital destiny, in the name of Jesus.

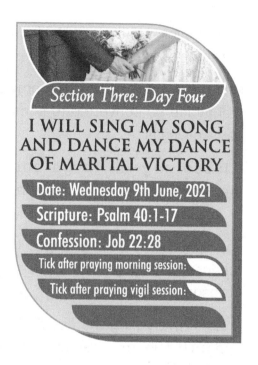

Section Three: Day Four

I WILL SING MY SONG AND DANCE MY DANCE OF MARITAL VICTORY

Date: Wednesday 9th June, 2021

Scripture: Psalm 40:1-17

Confession: Job 22:28

Tick after praying morning session:

Tick after praying vigil session:

PRAYERS FOR MORNING SESSION

1. Oh Lord, let every device of the enemy against my marital destiny be frustrated, in the name of Jesus.

2. Every force, scaring away my marriage partner, fall down and die in the name of Jesus.

3. I break every evil covenant working against my marital destiny, in the name of Jesus.

4. I destroy by fire, every demonic instrument fashioned against my marriage and destiny, in the name of Jesus.

5. All boasting powers delegated against my marriage, be silenced in the name of Jesus.

6. I withdraw my marriage from the hands of the oppressors, in the name of Jesus.

7. Every power chasing away my divine helpers, die in the name of Jesus.

8. Oh Lord, let heavenly fire ignite my marital life, in the name of Jesus.

9. Oh Lord, let the anointing for marital breakthrough fall powerfully on me, in the name of Jesus.

10. Oh Lord, give me divine prescription to my marital problems today, in the name of Jesus.

VIGIL PRAYERS

11. I receive power to overcome obstacles to my marital breakthroughs, in the name of Jesus.

12. Oh Lord, anoint my eyes to see divine vision, in the name of Jesus.

13. My marriage shall not be in struggle but in prosperity, in the name of Jesus.

14. O Lord let this year be the end of my stubborn marital pharaoh, in the name of Jesus.

15. O Lord, my father let not my name disappear from your book of remembrance this year. in the name of Jesus

16. Let the confidence of the wicked against my marital life this year be broken asunder, in the name of Jesus

17. Any evil hand that will point against my marriage and destiny this year shall dry up, in the name of Jesus.

18. Lord, forgive me for any wrong decision or wrong action or thought, that I engaged in, in the name of Jesus

19. Lord, give unto me the Eagle eye and eyes of Elisha to foresee marital problems. in the name of Jesus

20. Lord, help me to erect safeguards to prevent marriage break up. in the name of Jesus

Section Three: Day Five

I WILL SING MY SONG AND DANCE MY DANCE OF MARITAL VICTORY

Date: Thursday 10th June, 2021

Scripture: Psalm 134: 1-22

Confession: Psalm 2:4

Tick after praying morning session:

Tick after praying vigil session:

PRAYERS FOR MORNING SESSION

1. Every power keeping me low maritally, fall down and die, in the name of Jesus.

2. Let the rock and fire of God destroy every weapon of demotion fashioned against me maritally, in the name of Jesus.

3. I overrule every demonic decision made against my marital elevation, in the name of Jesus.

4. No evil meeting summoned against my marriage shall prosper, in the name of Jesus.

5. Let my youth be renewed like the eagle's, in the name of Jesus

6. Every satanic plan to embarrass me maritally be dissolved by fire, in the name of Jesus.

7. Every seed of poverty in my life, be roasted to ashes in the name of Jesus.

8. I reject every invitation to the arena of marital poverty, in the name of Jesus.

9. Every bad habit controlling my life, loose your hold over my life. in the name of Jesus

10. You, my marriage, receive fire, come forth, in the name of Jesus.

VIGIL PRAYERS

11. O God that never fails, settle me maritally to the shame of my enemies because it is my turn to laugh, in the name of Jesus.

12. By the power in the blood of Jesus, I neutralize every incantation working against my life, in the name of Jesus.

13. I revoke and nullify every witchcraft manipulation affecting my marriage, in the name of Jesus.

14. I curse every satanically sponsored disease germ working against my life to die, in the name of Jesus.

15. O God, arise and scatter every conspiracy working against my marriage, in the name of Jesus.

16. O God, arise and confuse the tongue of my stubborn enemies, in the name of Jesus.

17. I bind and cast away every spirit of fear and worry in my marriage, in the name of Jesus.

18. O God arise and speak healing and creative miracles into my marital life, in the name of Jesus.

19. My Father, release Your angels to fight my battles maritally, in the name of Jesus.

20. Father, let Your resurrection power come upon my marital life now, in the name of Jesus.

I WILL SING MY SONG AND DANCE MY DANCE OF MARITAL VICTORY

Date: Friday 11th June, 2021

Scripture: Psalm 135:1-28

Confession: Ezekiel 21:27

Tick after praying morning session:

Tick after praying vigil session:

PRAYERS FOR MORNING SESSION

1. I bind and cast out powers in charge of constant attacks and pain in my marital life, in the name of Jesus.

2. I destroy the communication gadget of darkness used against my marriage, in the name of Jesus.

3. Every charm working against my marital life, be destroyed, in the name of Jesus.

4. By the power in the blood of Jesus, I neutralise every arrow or incantation working against my marital life, in the name of Jesus.

5. I revoke and nullify every witchcraft manipulation affecting my marital life, in the name of Jesus.

6. I bind and cast out every negative influence of grave yard spirit upon my life in the name of Jesus.

7. O Lord cleanse my hand of every spot of relationship failure, in the Jesus.

8. Whatever the enemies say would be impossible with my hands, you my hands, hear the word of the Lord, begin to perform the impossible, in the name of Jesus.

9. O Lord prosper me beyond my wildest imaginations in Jesus name.

10. Yoke of satanic delay on my marital breakthrough, break, in the name of Jesus.

VIGIL PRAYERS

11. Every unseen fire, burning in my marital life, die, in the name of Jesus.

12. O finger of God, arise, command my lifting up, in the name of Jesus.

13. Well of prosperity, open unto me speedily, in the name of Jesus.

14. Every gate of brass in my dreams, break in the name of Jesus.

15. Any dream that does not originate from the Holy Ghost assigned to confuse me martially, die, in the name of Jesus.

16. Every stubborn enemy of my destiny, drawing their powers from the forest to attack my marital life and destiny, consuming fire of God, consume them and their forest. in the name of Jesus

17. Every satanic satellite and computer that the enemy is using to monitor each step of my marital life, explode and burn to ashes by the thunder fire of God. in the name of Jesus

18. Let my marital breakthrough and testimony appear and locate me by fire. in the name of Jesus

19. I recover back in seven folds all that the enemies have stolen from my marital life, in the name of Jesus.

20. Let as many as are stubborn and unrepentant against my marital congratulation be smitten by the sun in the day and by the moon in the night, in the name of Jesus.

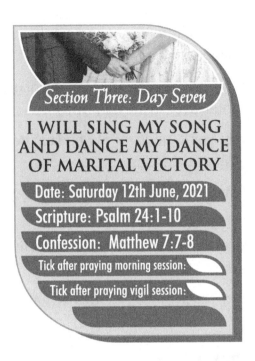

I WILL SING MY SONG AND DANCE MY DANCE OF MARITAL VICTORY

Date: Saturday 12th June, 2021

Scripture: Psalm 24:1-10

Confession: Matthew 7:7-8

Tick after praying morning session:

Tick after praying vigil session:

PRAYERS FOR MORNING SESSION

1. Let my spiritual eyes and ears be wide open, in the name of Jesus.

2. Spirit of the living God, quicken the whole of my being, in the name of Jesus.

3. Let the Holy Ghost smash my pride, in the name of Jesus.

4. In the name of Jesus, I capture every power behind my spiritual marital blindness and deafness.

5. Let my spiritual sight and ear drum receive healing, in the name of Jesus.

6. Holy Spirit, rain on me now rain of glory and marital favor, in the name of Jesus.

7. Holy Spirit, uncover my darkest secrets in the name of Jesus.

8. Holy Spirit fire, ignite me to the glory of God, in the name of Jesus.

9. Let my spirit man become divine fire, in the name of Jesus.

10. Lord, teach me to be crucified with you.

VIGIL PRAYERS

11. Let not your peace depart from me, O Lord.

12. O Lord, let the spirit that flees from sin incubate my life.

13. I claim all my marital rights now, in the name of Jesus.

14. I release my money from the house of the strong man, in the name of Jesus.

15. Let the power of God pull down the strongholds of the enemies of my marital life, in the name of Jesus.

16. Every power preventing the perfect will of God from being done in my life, receive failure and defeat, in the name of Jesus.

17. Every demon hindering, delaying, preventing, destroying and breaking my marital testimony, receive confusion, in the name of Jesus.

18. Every band of the wicked that is arresting my marital testimony break, in the name of Jesus.

19. O God, arise and make me laugh my enemies to scorn, in the name of Jesus.

20. O God, arise with all your weapons of war and fight my marriage to manifestation for me this year, in the name of Jesus.

TESTIMONIES

Encourage yourself with few testimonies of singles who had participated in previous editions of this annual prayer and fasting programme and are now happily married to the glory of God.

Before I proceed, I will like to ask for God's forgiveness and mercy for staying this long before sharing this testimony. I always attend all MFM Gen218 singles programs and during the annual fasting and prayer programmes, I made a promise that if God should answer me I will come back to testify. I told God to give me a special 40th birthday gift which was to come up on the 28th of August, that the special birthday gift should be a marriage proposal, and to God be the glory my husband proposed to me on the 27th of July, not long after we ended the fasting program. And we got married on October 15th. Glory be to God for His faithfulness. Praise God.

Sis. Mercy

Good afternoon sir/madam,

We want to return praise unto our Maker and Sustainer and also bless the name of the Lord for what God did for me and my husband. I diligently participated in the 2019 MFM Gen218 Annual Fasting and Prayer program and now.

God has changed my marital status, He wiped away my tears and I got married in April, 2021. This is God's doing and it is marvelous in our eyes. I return all the glory to God. I'm short of words to express my joy. Praise the Lord!

Mrs. Olugbenga

Praise God!

God never fails. I have always participated in the MFM Gen218 Annual Fasting and Prayer Program. But in 2018, I was almost giving up on marriage because I have been praying hard for years. Marriage seems not to be forthcoming and I was almost clocking to 40years. There were nights that I would cry secretly but I kept praying. I kept listening to several messages of our Father-in-the-Lord, Dr. D. K. Olukoya and I increased my habit of singing praises and worship to God as well as Bible reading.

Early 2019, I completely gave up on marriage and consoled myself. I became active in my Region and I kept serving God. But when they announced the Annual Fasting and Prayer program for 2019, I told God that I'm giving Him a last chance to answer me maritally, that I do not want to participate in the next edition as a single. So I made sure that I fasted and prayed diligently, I sang praises to God after my prayers. Beloved, like a dream, God connected me to my husband; it happened like a surpise to me and we got married last year. God has also blessed us with a baby boy. I thank God for the ministry of Dr. D.K. Olukoya and the MFM Gen218 Ministry

Praise the Lord

Sis. Jenn

My relationship got broken after we had known both parents and were about to start marriage processes. The lady was to go to UK for her masters program and we were supposed to wed immediately after. Getting to UK, she sent a message that she's no longer interested and that I shouldn't relate the news with her family till she returns.

I felt so bad after I got the news and then had thought I may not marry a Christian lady.

I participated in the Gen218 annual fasting and

prayer program that faithful year, and God gave me a name in capital letter. I began to look for the owner of the name, till the day I prayed to the Holy Spirit to bring this person my way. The prayer didn't wait for an hour before she surfaced. We became friends and by God's grace, our marriage will be 4 years next month. Praise the Lord

Bro. Lanre

Before I proceed, I will like to ask for God's forgiveness and mercy for staying this long before sharing this testimony. I never took the annual Gen218 fasting program for granted but after several years I was beginning to loose hope. I always attend all Gen218 singles programs at Prayer City and in Lagos. At a point I felt maybe God did not want me to marry because I have been waiting for too long, but whenever Daddy G.O. prays for singles, I feel hope again.

So in 2019, I entered a covenant with God and told Him that before the 2nd quarter of the year 2020, He should perfect all that concerns my marriage and by my next birthday which is November I want to carry my baby. Although along the line I got discouraged but I encouraged myself in the Lord, although it was difficult o.

Today, the God of wonders proved Himself, early February 2020, I met my husband and by June 2020 we got married. The Covenant keeping God who never fails, that same year I conceived and gave birth in this year without any delay at all.Glory be to God for His faithfulness. Praise God.

Sis. Mariam

The programme shall be rounded off with a Marathon prayer meeting with our Father in the Lord, Dr D. K. Olukoya on the last day of the programme, Saturday June 12th 2021 by 8.00am, at the MFM International Headquarters, Onike, Yaba. It will be streamed live at our major Regional Headquarters nationwide and on all our online platforms.

  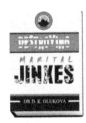 

Made in the USA
Middletown, DE
20 May 2021